ENTREPRENEURSHIP FOR
HUMAN FLOURISHING

ENTREPRENEURSHIP FOR HUMAN FLOURISHING

Chris Horst and Peter Greer
HOPE International

AEI Press
Washington, D.C.

Distributed by arrangement with the National Book Network, 15200 NBN Way, Blue Ridge Summit, PA 17214. To order, call toll-free 1-800-462-6420 or 1-717-794-3800.

For all other inquiries, please contact AEI Press, 1150 17th Street, NW, Washington, DC 20036, or call 202-862-5916.

Library of Congress Cataloging-in-Publication Data

Greer, Peter, 1975-
  Entrepreneurship for human flourishing / Peter Greer, Chris Horst.
  pages cm
  Includes bibliographical references and index.
  ISBN 978-0-8447-7267-7 (pbk.)
  ISBN 978-0-8447-7268-4 (ebook)
  1. Poverty—Religious aspects—Christianity. 2. Social entrepreneurship.
  3. Social responsibility of business. I. Title.
  BV4647.P6G737 2009
  261.8'325—dc23

                                                    2014012778

CONTENTS

FOREWORD

The eminent sociologist Peter Berger once described the United States as a nation of Indians ruled by Swedes. By this, he meant that ordinary Americans are a vibrantly religious people, akin to India with its practicing Hindus, Buddhists, Muslims, Christians, and others. Gallup has been surveying Americans since 1944 to ask if they believe in God, and every year more than 9 in 10 have said yes.

But many cultural and political elites in the United States do not share this religiosity. Berger compares these "rulers" to the Swedish, of whom fewer than 18 percent profess divine belief and less than 4 percent attend weekly religious services.

In the academy, we can see both dynamics at work. Many Ivy League and other elite schools were founded long ago for the express purpose of advancing Christian theology and learning. Yet today new allegiances have replaced these founding purposes. The rise of science and an Enlightenment-based commitment to reason have often been accompanied by distaste for religious faith. In many contemporary academic departments, race, gender, and class have become lenses through which history and contemporary affairs are understood.

Of course, not all college campuses have followed this path. As of 2014, more than 900 of America's approximately 1,700 private, four-year colleges are religious schools. Of these, 119 are evangelical colleges that qualify for membership in the Council for Christian Colleges and Universities because of their particular views of Scripture and historic Christian doctrine.

This book was written with these faith-based campuses squarely in mind. Since 2009, the American Enterprise Institute—through its Values & Capitalism project—has built a special outreach initiative to Christian colleges throughout the United States to advance a moral case for free enterprise in partnership with professors and students.

While views on these campuses are by no means monolithic about markets and the role of the state in regulating the economy, one shared conviction at virtually all evangelical campuses is that work comes from God—and is therefore a gift. Work was assigned to Adam and Eve in the Garden of Eden, before the fall. The mandate to steward the earth and to bear the *imago dei* by exercising dominion throughout the created order means that in spite of sin, work is an essential and inherent part of what it means to be human.

In fact, Jesus Christ embodied this insight during his life on earth. As the moral philosopher and theologian Michael Novak recently observed, "The Lord God Creator called the Christ, the Redeemer, to shoulder the vocation of small business: a creative vocation, a vocation of humble service . . . helping his family earn its own way."[1] It is all too easy to miss the reality that Jesus was a hardworking entrepreneur; remarkably, theologian Klaus Issler estimates that Jesus spent six times as many years working as a carpenter as he did in his public ministry.[2]

This fact should help Christians take heart and be inspired to discover and put to use our unique, God-given talents in the workplace, because this is what we were made to do.

As Chris Horst and Peter Greer describe in this volume, entrepreneurship is often difficult because it involves personal risk, new territory, and typically trial and error. And yet the Christian entrepreneur can be guided not only by life experience but also by faith. Entrepreneurs who live by faith can put into practice the reality many Christian colleges today teach: that there is no sacred-secular divide and that Sunday morning faith is no different than that which sustains one's 40-hour workweek.

This book deepens this insight by combining first-rate scholarship with the power of true, first-hand stories. Moreover, the authors explain how entrepreneurial capitalism is the long-term hope of the poor—and, therefore, of us all.

If you are a Christian college student, or if you are considering a leap of faith as an entrepreneur, this AEI book is written particularly with you in mind. I hope it can help you to think anew about the value of entrepreneurship and to persevere in the challenging work of discerning your own vocation. Although that journey is sometimes a struggle, it is also a joy-filled journey—particularly because, in the context of business, we can emulate the Creator by bringing into being new goods and services that can bless people and foster human flourishing.

—*Josh Good, AEI Values & Capitalism Program Manager*

1

INTRODUCTION

I (Chris) walked through the doors of the exhibition hall, excited about the Denver Faith and Justice Conference. Throughout the event, I could feel the energy generated by hundreds of young leaders passionate about fighting global poverty and injustice. But something was missing.

Peter and I are privileged to participate in many conferences and conversations on justice and poverty. Over the years, we've developed the habit of scouring speaker lists. While looking at lineups of plenary and breakout presenters is not odd in itself, the peculiar nature of our habit is that we vocation hunt. Specifically, we search for businesspeople.

Like prospectors in a stream, we sift through programs to find that rare deposit of gold—a presenter with a direct connection to business. Typically, it's a *social* entrepreneur of some variety. It could be a businessperson employing homeless people or teaching recovering addicts a new skill. Or someone who has started a business overseas to employ women escaping prostitution. Or an entrepreneur who *left* business to use his skills with a nonprofit. Or a business owner selling scarce resources in a particularly vulnerable neighborhood—like a grocer opening up shop in an urban "food desert." These people look a lot like our colleagues serving in HOPE International's microfinance programs around the world.

But it is uncommon to find an everyday

businessperson at a justice conference. That particular weekend in October, the Denver Faith and Justice Conference was no different. Despite an impressive lineup, not a single businessperson was on the speaker list.

Despite attending dozens of such conferences over the years, we've yet to hear from a metal manufacturer or commercial banker, a homebuilder or tax accountant. That doesn't make sense. If we are truly committed to justice and poverty eradication, then we simply must learn to celebrate the powerful impact of "normal" everyday businessmen and businesswomen. This book will show you why.

In this book, we explore entrepreneurship in all its stages—small, big, and grassroots—and articulate how essential it is for vibrant economies and flourishing communities. Chapter Two builds the case for the centrality of enterprise in the war on poverty. Chapter Three examines the role of small and medium-sized businesses. Chapter Four investigates mature enterprises—global multinational corporations. Chapter Five explores entrepreneurship at the grassroots level. Chapter Six discusses the insufficiency of financial success alone and the key roles faith and values play in human flourishing.

Woven throughout each chapter are stories of remarkable men and women who create, build, and understand the high calling they have to live as entrepreneurs—people we hope you might one day see featured at a justice conference for their work in alleviating poverty and promoting flourishing communities.

2

THE FLOURISHING OF PEOPLE AND PLACES

We both grew up in church. Sunday mornings frequently found us listening to missionaries' updates. Years of inspirational missionary stories and justice conferences have left us amazed by efforts of remarkable people serving in challenging places. We are fortunate to call many of these creative and courageous people friends. They're an inspiration.

But they represent just a tiny slice of the global workforce. Unintentionally, our fixation on a few has sidelined entrepreneurs and those who work in business. It has relegated businesspeople to the role of cheerleaders. In our culture, businesspeople are told to work hard and give generously—and then get out of the way for the "real" work of the nonprofit activists, missionaries, and pastors. This vocational king-making tacitly communicates that only those working in social enterprises are involved in the issues of poverty and injustice.

But after looking at the data about what transforms poverty-stricken communities in a lasting way, we have come to the conclusion that if you care about helping the poor, you simply must care about business and entrepreneurship. Nonprofit organizations play important roles in flourishing societies, but they work only if they are supplementing a vibrant business community.

As Wayne Grudem and Barry Asmus argue in *The Poverty of Nations*: "Businesses produce, distribute, and sell trillions of dollars worth of goods around the world every year. And businesses provide the vast majority of jobs that pay people for their work and provide a market in which products can be sold."[3]

Business is not secondary in helping the poor; it is primary. Ultimately, we need a broader understanding of the influence of commerce and entrepreneurship, one that celebrates and affirms the potential of everyday businesspeople. We must not, of course, overlook the villains and the cronyism contorting the marketplace for ill-gotten gains. But we must see these as the crooked exceptions, not the norm. In this marketplace, entrepreneurs and those they employ each serve a valuable role—financial advisers, graphic designers, accountants, and electrical engineers alike. And they are contributing more to solving the world's problems than they likely assume.

Before exploring the reasons why entrepreneurship is essential for human flourishing, we want to be clear about our definitions.

ENTREPRENEURSHIP
Entrepreneurship occurs when people use their God-given skills and abilities to create and grow organizations. It's real estate developers who construct and manage buildings where people live and work. It's tailors who create jackets and jeans. It's

engineering firms designing systems to recycle wastewater.

Not all entrepreneurship is good, of course. We've all heard stories about companies that take advantage of their workers or cut corners when it comes to environmental practices. Casinos, prostitution, and drug sales can have a corrosive effect on our neighborhoods, and unscrupulous varieties of legal and illegal entrepreneurship blight communities.

But immoral businesses lack staying power. Eventually, like the failed energy titan Enron and the once-popular car company Yugo, these companies will collapse or be shut down for infractions. A company operating outside legal bounds or victimizing its employees or customers will have a very short life.

In general, entrepreneurs are in the business of solving problems, not creating them. Their initiatives and inventions—and the businesses that sustain them—meet human needs. Tables allow families to share meals together. Telephones enable friends to communicate in real time. Airplanes permit people to travel the globe.

Tables, telephones, and airplanes are handicrafts of entrepreneurs. When entrepreneurs fulfill their mandate to serve others and solve problems, humans flourish. And to solve these problems, entrepreneurs recruit workers, who can also then experience the dignity of work. At its best, entrepreneurship aims to encourage human flourishing.

HUMAN FLOURISHING

Human flourishing goes beyond the absence of poverty. There's a difference between a "not empty" life and a "full" one. It's not easy to define living life to its fullest. Anthony Bradley, professor of theology and ethics at The King's College, describes it this way: "[It is] characterized by a holistic concern for the spiritual, moral, physical, economic, material, political, psychological, and social context necessary for human beings to live according to their design."[4]

The ancient Hebrew word *shalom* goes beyond our modern concept of peace and embodies completeness in relationships with God, others, ourselves, and creation.[5] Human flourishing happens when people and communities thrive—when they experience wholeness and restoration in their relationships, in their view of themselves, and in their relationship with their Creator.

Entrepreneurship is integral to human flourishing. When a city or country lacks employers and businesses, crime, drug abuse, prostitution, and hardship swell. Where there is an abundance of entrepreneurship, employment rises—and human benefits extend beyond the provision of material goods and services alone.

Michael Novak summarizes, "How can we quickly discern the health of a nation? It's easy: Look at how many small businesses were created in the last year. If the number is high, the society is typically on the rise. If it's low, we know the nation is headed for trouble. Entrepreneurship reflects what is happening in the culture."[6]

HAPPINESS, PEACE, AND PROSPERITY

Using the Gallup-Healthways Well-Being Index, Richard Florida shows the connection between employment and well-being in his March 2011 essay for the *Atlantic*. In Florida's analysis, the index accounts for "life evaluation, emotional health, work environment, physical health, healthy behaviors, and access to basic necessities."[7]

"Are wealthier cities, like wealthier nations, also happier cities?" Florida asks. "Indeed they are. We find reasonably strong correlations between well-being and several measures of income and wealth. . . . Conventional wisdom and academic studies alike suggest that levels of happiness would fall as unemployment rises. And this is what we find."

This same reality is true for prosperous countries. Freer markets and higher levels of meaningful employment translate to higher levels of life satisfaction.[8] Said plainly, people are more likely to flourish as entrepreneurship increases. This belief might seem common sense. But the dearth of entrepreneurs speaking at justice conferences communicates that it still is not commonly held. Entrepreneurs are viewed as secondary, not central, to the war on poverty.

Beyond boosting personal satisfaction for an individual, entrepreneurship is also a pillar of safe and harmonious societies. "Capitalism and economic freedom promote peace," writes Professor Erich Weede.[9]

In Weede's research on the relationship between globalization, economic growth, and violence, he discovered how vibrant markets promote peace. The starkest proof of Weede's findings is in places where two opposing strategies existed side by side: for example, the not-so-distant disparities between East Germany and West Germany.

Or, today, examine the differences in poverty, peace, and safety between South Korea and North Korea. North Korea is shielded from the outside world. The hard-fisted North Korean regime prohibits journalists and economists from assessing the realities for the North Korean people. But we know enough to realize that misery and poverty is widespread, reaching levels unmatched anywhere else in the world. South Korea, on the other hand, is the 13th richest country in the world.[10] Not that long ago, this contrast did not exist.

"Around the time of Mao Zedong's death (1976), North Korea was more educated, more productive and (by the measure of international trade per capita) much more open than China," writes political economist Nicholas Eberstadt. "Around that same time, in fact, per capita output in North Korea and South Korea may have been quite similar. Today, North Korea has the awful distinction of being the only literate and urbanized society in human history to suffer mass famine in peacetime."[11]

Today, South Korea boasts one of the world's healthiest economies. Homemade power brands like Samsung, Hyundai, and LG employ millions of South Koreans in high-paying jobs and produce valuable products sold across the world. North Korea imports and exports virtually nothing. Though it's likely (no reliable data exists) a high percentage of North Koreans have "jobs"—a core promise of a centrally planned government—this faux employment does not pay well enough to put food on the table. In his book *The Coming Jobs War,* Jim Clifton, CEO of Gallup, looked at Gallup's volumes of global research and came to this conclusion: the most significant global issue in our time—more pressing than even terrorism or environmental degradation—is job creation. "If countries fail at creating jobs," says Clifton, "their societies will fall apart. Countries, and more specifically cities, will experience suffering, instability, chaos, and eventually revolution."[12]

When thinking about how to help the hurting and vulnerable flourish, our minds race to the tangible solutions of most immediate help for people in crisis. We think of charitable organizations like food banks and homeless shelters. There is good reason for that. Charities play a crucial role in society, serving the down-and-out and protecting the interests of the vulnerable. But charity is at its best when it complements the private sector, when it *temporarily* assists those who are unable to participate in productive employment and take care of themselves and their families.

In advancing the flourishing of all people, it's easy to forget the key role of entrepreneurship. Business is the engine of human flourishing. And businesses are where most adults spend the majority of their time. Through that lens, entrepreneurship is clearly more than a means to increase shareholder value or to make a living. When students return from service trips to countries in Africa and South America, many often reflect that the people they met seemed happy despite their limited possessions. And, certainly, possessions alone do not produce happiness.

But prosperity directly influences mental stability. In a study of global depression rates, researchers at Australia's University of Queensland found that conflict, high unemployment, and low incomes drive up rates of clinically diagnosed depression. In poor regions like sub-Saharan Africa and the Middle East, depression rates are far higher than in North America, Europe, and high-income countries in Asia.[13] Rates of depression, peace, and happiness are key metrics underscoring an important point: good jobs matter—a lot.

John Perkins, a heroic civil rights activist, pastor, and contemporary of Martin Luther King Jr., once said, "Jobs are the world's best social service program."[14] An authority on the plight of America's vulnerable, Perkins understands that meaningful work isn't just *a* solution to the problem of financially vulnerable people. It's *the* best solution.

MONOTONY AND AMBIGUITY

Of course, "entrepreneurship for human flourishing" can read well on paper, but business can still be drudgery for many workers. Regardless of the talent of entrepreneurs or the ingenuity of their innovations, workers still can feel unfulfilled.

In a study of more than 100 million American workers, Gallup found that just 30 percent of workers are emotionally engaged in their responsibilities.[15] If we do not recapture a restored vision of vocation, broadly, and of entrepreneurship, specifically, we will continue to see disengaged employees.

We'll also lack the jobs, products, and services needed for flourishing communities.

On the other hand, millions of workers sustain innovative businesses today. And these are businesses built to solve major societal problems. Economist Arthur Brooks has noted that a stark difference exists between being engaged and being satisfied with daily work. Approximately 80 percent of Americans say they are fairly, very, or completely satisfied with their work.[16]

So it may be that American workers are satisfied with, but not emotionally invested in, their jobs. Why is that? It's partly because contemporary Verizon store managers, Apple iPhone developers, or Southwest Airlines flight attendants can feel distanced from what Alexander Graham Bell, Steve Jobs, and Orville Wright experienced in first creating the products sold at local stores. It's difficult to make that correlation when stuck in what can feel like a mundane job, such as selling phone plans or tracking accounts payable for a massive airline conglomerate.

Because we both raise money for a nonprofit, we interact with businesspeople every day. These donors, board members, and investors are the ones who make it possible for us to serve and support entrepreneurs working in conditions of extreme poverty across the globe.

Sadly, it's become very normal to hear our friends lament that their work feels insignificant. We've listened to insulin sales representatives, medical device manufacturers, and commercial bankers grieve that their jobs aren't having an impact in comparison to ours. "If only I could do work that mattered, like you," we've heard many times over. In their words, we're out saving the world, while they're simply making widgets and earning paychecks.

Where does this idea germinate? How have we minimized the impact of people providing drugs like insulin, which enables individuals with diabetes to live normal lives? Or downplayed the calling of the individual who created the pacemaker that saved a grandmother's life? Or neglected to celebrate the banker who facilitated the investment in a business that provided employment for a father of four?

In fact, our economy fits together like an ecosystem, even though it can feel as if a tax status (nonprofit versus for-profit) validates some vocations while demeaning others. In the *Wall Street Journal*, Paul Rubin, professor of economics at Emory University, said the way we frame our conversation about economics undersells its power for good: "Economists originally borrowed the competition metaphor from sports, events that exist to choose winners and losers. But in economics, everyone can win from exchange. . . . People would feel much more favorably toward a 'cooperative economy' than a 'competitive economy.'"[17]

Rubin believes the language of competition has inadvertently driven those both inside and outside business to miss the real reason businesses exist. Such language, accompanied by the Hollywood caricatures of dictatorial CEOs and greedy business owners, has provided a truncated perception of the role of entrepreneurship.

"The myth that profit maximization is the sole purpose of business has done enormous damage to the reputation of capitalism and the legitimacy of business in society," wrote John Mackey, founder and president of Whole Foods Market. "We need to recapture the narrative and restore it to its true essence: that the purpose of business is to improve our lives and to create value for stakeholders."[18]

Mackey understands that his role as a business owner is to create meaningful employment for thousands, provide healthy and high-quality food for customers, and serve communities. Today, Mackey employs over 70,000 people in 340 Whole Foods Markets worldwide. *Fortune* magazine lists Whole Foods as one of the top 100 companies to work for. His company is widely credited for the expansion of the organic, natural, and healthy food movement, filling American refrigerators and pantries with healthier and better foods.

But very few are aware that he began his company as a nonprofit co-op, because it was "based on cooperation instead of competition."[19] As a 20-something, Mackey was a self-described hippie. He had long hair, a full beard, and a firm distaste for business. "In contrast to evil corporations, I believed that nonprofit organizations and government were 'good,' because they altruistically worked for the public interest," wrote Mackey.[20]

But he soon became disillusioned with the co-op model—for a host of reasons—and realized the best way for him to accomplish his goals was to launch a for-profit grocery store. "I was still very much an idealist who wanted to make the world a better place," wrote Mackey, "and I thought I could best do so by operating a store that sold healthy food to people and provided good jobs."[21]

Today, he leads a company creating tremendous value for his investors, employees, farmers, landlords, customers, and communities. Mackey now realizes that what matters more than for-profit or nonprofit status is whether we are deploying our gifts and abilities for good. When we can see our jobs in light of their grander purposes, it translates the trivial into significant, the secular into sacred.

Christian essayist Dorothy Sayers describes work "not as a necessary drudgery to be undergone for the purpose of making money, but as a way of life in which the nature of man should find its proper exercise and delight and so fulfill itself to the glory of God."[22]

She writes, "It should, in fact, be thought of as a creative activity undertaken for the love of the work itself; and that man, made in God's image, should make things, as God makes them, for the sake of doing well a thing that is well worth doing."[23]

In the Christian story of creation, the very first action God took was to work. He created. As the master creator and entrepreneur, God brought order out of chaos. He brought life to a world "formless and void" (Gen. 1:2). And God concluded his work by crafting people—Adam and Eve—and said that his work was "very good."

The first command He gave to Adam and Eve was to work. He instructed them to cultivate the Garden of Eden, to steward the creation. This command came before the first bite into the fateful apple, so it was not a punishment. He gave them work as a gift, something He knew we were made for. And when we are deprived of the opportunity to work—willfully or not—we lose part of what makes us exhibit the image of the Divine.

That is why Christians, especially, cannot neglect entrepreneurship. Other institutions—governments, charities, and schools—can provide work, but only business is capable of creating and sustaining the jobs needed to employ masses of people and to create valuable products and services that society needs.

And of course, jobs can make an impact not just among America's vulnerable communities.

IS POVERTY DISAPPEARING?

The global surge in meaningful employment is changing the world. At a Georgetown University conference on poverty and entrepreneurship in November 2012, Bono—lead singer of U2 and advocate for the poor—admitted a "humbling realization" about the role of entrepreneurship and the private sector.[24] He previously had viewed commerce as the problem. Today, he sees it as the primary solution to poverty.

"[I'm a] rock-star preaching capitalism. Wow. Sometimes I hear myself and I just can't believe it. Commerce is real . . . aid is just a stopgap. Commerce—entrepreneurial capitalism—takes more people out of poverty than aid," said Bono.

Bono's acknowledgment is noteworthy. But the case for economic growth extends far beyond a celebrity anecdote. The verdict is in. By overwhelming margins, free markets have enabled more people to escape poverty than any other economic system in the history of the world.

Yale University and the Brookings Institution

FIGURE 1. GLOBAL POVERTY RATE, 1981–2011

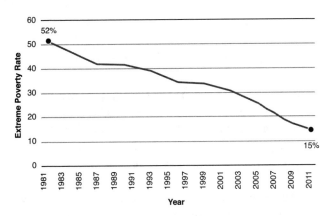

Source: World Bank

released a study in 2011 to join the chorus of research validating this claim.[25] According to their study, in 1981, 52 percent of the world's population was unable to provide for their basic needs, like housing and food, and was living below the "extreme poverty line." By the end of 2011, just 30 years later, that percentage plummeted to 15 percent. (See figure 1.) That was due not to the World Bank or the United Nations, but rather to the "rise of globalization and the spread of capitalism."

In an article entitled "Towards the End of Poverty," the *Economist* summarized the dramatic decrease of global poverty in this way:

> The world's achievement in the field of poverty reduction is, by almost any measure, impressive . . . the aim of halving global poverty between 1990 and 2015 was achieved five years early. Most of the credit, however, must go to capitalism and free trade, for they enable economies to grow—and it was growth, principally, that has eased destitution.[26]

Jobs are the central weapon in the war on poverty. They are the centerpiece of communities that flourish.[27]

COUNTERING THE STEREOTYPES

Winston Churchill once said, "Some see private enterprise as a predatory target to be shot, others as a cow to be milked, but few are those who see it as a sturdy horse pulling the wagon." Do young Americans believe business is a predator, a cow, or a horse?

From our informal inventory of justice conference speakers, we'd bet they think it's a cow, at best, or a predator, at worst. We do not believe that nonprofit individuals and activists should be excluded from speaking at these events, but we do think that

---

Jobs are the central weapon in the war on poverty.

---

our friends and colaborers whose hands are pulling the enterprise plow should share the stage.

Entrepreneurship is not something we should just tolerate. We should celebrate it. Average life expectancy has more than doubled globally over the past 200 years. During that time, we've moved from a nearly illiterate population to one in which 84 percent of adults can now read. In the past 40 years alone, the percentage of undernourished people in the world has dropped by half.[28]

This is very good news. According to Bono and the Yale researchers, entrepreneurs are on the front lines of this progress. Ordinary women and men doing ordinary work are actually achieving something extraordinary. The accumulated efforts of these hardworking individuals are changing the world.

This means all of us, not just social workers and missionaries, have a role to fulfill. As we've argued, entrepreneurship has a particularly central purpose in the flourishing of people and places. Without it, capital to invest in new ideas, civil society, and jobs for others is impossible to come by. In conversation with others, entrepreneurs and businesspeople need to realize and own the good and redemptive ways enterprise contributes to our communities.

3

THE HEART
AND SOUL OF
ENTREPRENEURSHIP

Adrian Groff could have pursued a job with one of the "Big Four" accounting firms. But he felt drawn to small business.

Often, his work isn't glamorous. "For those working in the trades, it's a dirty, sweaty job. . . . I mean, some of these guys on my plumbing team literally take care of crap," said Groff, vice president at Groff's Home Comfort Team.[29]

After graduating with a dual degree in accounting and management and completing a one-year business fellowship, Groff returned to his hometown of Lancaster, Pennsylvania, and joined the family business.

"The vision of carrying on the dreams of my father and his business partner was too important for me to let go," shared Groff. "I am a steward of Groff's family business, from serving our customers exceptionally well to providing an awesome place to work. From serving our customers with excellence to sharing the financial blessings and experiences of this business with our community."

A full-service construction firm, Groff's Home Comfort Team is capable of building or repairing any system in the house. The company builds home lighting arrangements and troubleshoots when dishwashers or toilets are malfunctioning. But at the core, the mission is even simpler.

"We make things work," said Groff. "We use our

knowledge to make things work more efficiently and better for everyone."

There's a reason 65 percent of Americans place a high level of confidence in small business.[30] They recognize that services like Groff's are critical to their neighborhoods. In this chapter, we'll explore how small businesses act as the frontline defense against poverty.

MIGHTY SMALL BUSINESS

Globally, a small business is understood to be a for-profit organization employing between 5 and 500 employees. There are countless varieties of small businesses, but what's definitive is their economic importance.

In high-income countries, more than half of the gross domestic product (GDP) is generated by and more than 60 percent of workers are employed by small businesses.[31] According to the US Small Business Administration, small businesses are also a key component in net job growth. For example, the United States alone has 29 million small businesses, accounting for 60 to 80 percent of all new jobs.[32] Between 1980 and 2000, more than five million jobs disappeared at Fortune 500 companies. During that same time, however, more than 34 million new jobs were created almost entirely as a result of American small business.[33]

In a study on the effect of small business on economic growth and poverty alleviation, researchers Gebremeskel Gebremariam, Tesfa Gebremedhin, and Randall Jackson explain:

> It is now well accepted both among academicians and policy makers that small businesses play a vital role in contributing to the overall economic performance of countries. . . . [They] play an important role in community development by enticing private investment back into lagging areas and spread the benefits of economic growth to people and places too often left behind. Through their capital investments, private small businesses and micro-enterprises create jobs and new opportunities that promote community-building and social activities.[34]

In West Virginia, the focus of their study, they found "a strong link between small business development, economic growth and poverty alleviation. An increase in the percentage share of small business employment had a positive impact on economic growth and consequently reduced poverty in West Virginia from 1980 to 2001."[35]

Groff's is a quintessential illustration of these findings. Adrian Groff's father started the business in his garage in 1988 with the goal of employing as many people as possible. But he didn't want to provide just a paycheck. Rather, he wanted to create a work environment where all his workers were treated with dignity and respect.

Groff's celebrated its 25th anniversary in 2013. Today, the company employs more than 70 plumbers, electricians, and estimators. The owners strive to take care of all their stakeholders—their employees, customers, owners, and community. And as you begin peeling back the layers of the Groff's business, it's easy to see why companies like Groff's are vital to the flourishing of our communities.

Each of the 70 employees represents a family. Groff's provides livelihoods to these families and allows them to purchase homes, put food on the table, and invest in their communities. Corporately, Groff's donates time and money to local schools and sponsors charity events.

But more importantly, it fulfills its core mission with excellence. The company helps homeowners find efficiencies to save costs and reduce energy usage. It provides trusted advice to landlords who face chronic plumbing issues and assesses the costs of electrical upgrades. Groff's is a reliable and affordable partner for homeowners. The business makes things work, which is its very reason for existing.

When a community lacks companies like Groff's,

people suffer. And it's even worse when entire countries lack small businesses.

THE MISSING MIDDLE

There's a direct correlation between the ease of opening a small business and a region's prosperity.

In *The Spirit of Democratic Capitalism,* Michael Novak argues that the free market has the most significant role in fostering human flourishing: "Of all the systems of political economy which have shaped our history, none has so revolutionized ordinary expectations of human life—lengthened the life span, made the elimination of poverty and famine thinkable, enlarged the range of human choice—as democratic capitalism."[36]

Novak's assertion is further substantiated by poverty rates in the United States, examined over the last decade by the Goldwater Institute. When looking at the top states, the institute found, "Economic freedom and entrepreneurship are keys to escaping poverty for many. There is a strong connection between a state's rate of entrepreneurship and declines in poverty."[37]

Since 2003, the World Bank has been publishing its *Ease of Doing Business* report, which ranks every country based on the ease of registering a new business, levels of business taxation, reliability of the power grid, and degree of corruption, among other

---

There's a direct correlation between the ease of opening a small business and a region's prosperity.

---

variables. The analysis is compelling: "Enabling growth—and ensuring that all people, regardless of income level, can participate in its benefits—requires an environment where new entrants with drive and good ideas can get started in business and where good firms can invest and grow, thereby generating more jobs."[38]

To combat poverty, countries must open their borders to trade and make the business climate conducive and welcoming to entrepreneurs. In developing countries, specifically, businesses provide an estimated 90 percent of all jobs.[39] Leaders who recognize these realities have aggressively positioned their policies accordingly.

Although the private sector provides the bulk of jobs in these countries, the jobs are concentrated at either end of the business spectrum. Massive companies and informal, grassroots businesses are strong, but there is a gaping hole in between.

When Harvard professor Asim Khwaja examined global data on small business, he found that high-income countries had a much higher percentage of

FIGURE 2. FIRM SIZE DISTRIBUTION

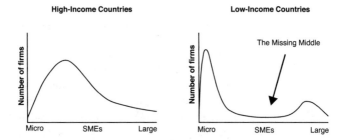

Note: SMEs = small and medium enterprises.
Source: Center for International Development, Harvard University.

small firms than low-income countries. In comparison, small companies in low-income countries provide less than half the benefit to communities of their high-income counterparts. As we have mentioned, in high-income countries, more than 50 percent of the GDP and more than 60 percent of workers are employed through small businesses.

However, in low-income countries, small businesses supply just 17 percent of GDP and employ 30 percent of the workforce.[40] This is the "missing middle." There is a gaping hole in low-income countries where small and medium-sized businesses should be. (See figure 2.)

In a mature economy like the United States, we need businesspeople to continue starting and growing small businesses. High rates of entrepreneurship and small business are crucial to human flourishing. And beyond our borders, the stakes are even higher. A growing number of businesspeople are attempting to transform the "missing middle" in lower-income countries into the engine that powers their economies.

CLOSING THE GAP

Henry Kaestner is a risk taker. An entrepreneur from Durham, North Carolina, he is looking to close the gap between high- and low-income countries through the influence of small business.

Kaestner dreams big and has an exceptional knack for a good business idea. One of his first businesses was Bandwidth, a telecommunications company he cofounded in 1999. Bandwidth grew from a successful small business to a major national telecommunications powerhouse: today, it grosses more than $140 million annually and employs more than 550 people across multiple states.[41] After seeing the value his company added to Durham, Kaestner aspired to see that gain replicated across the globe.[42]

In 2011, he launched Sovereign's Capital, a global small-business investment and consulting firm. Sovereign's focus is to invest in early growth–stage companies in emerging markets, and its portfolio includes companies operating in Nepal, Indonesia, and China.

CloudFactory, based in Kathmandu, Nepal, is one company in which Sovereign's is investing. Located in a country with a 46 percent unemployment rate, the company hires software engineers to process and aggregate data, like a virtual assembly line. The market for such technology services is massive, and today CloudFactory is poised to become one of the biggest employers in Nepal.

It's early, but Kaestner is starting to see the impact of Sovereign's investments in these top-shelf small businesses. "We believe small businesses are the lifeblood of every economy," shared Kaestner. "It's where creativity and innovation happens. We believe entrepreneurial ventures make the greatest impact on the leaders of economies tomorrow."

Healthy communities boast flourishing business environments. In these places, both small companies like Groff's and large companies like Bandwidth employ individuals and generate the revenue and services healthy societies need.

4

VISIONARY LEADER-SHIP AND THE SOUL OF BIG BUSINESS

Elyse Bealer is a member of the Cherokee Nation. Her ancestors walked the Trail of Tears as part of the Indian Removal Act of 1830, which forced them to move west. They were escorted by the US Army from North Carolina to Oklahoma. They were among the few who survived the journey.[43]

Bealer understands the plight of the vulnerable in America. The Cherokee Nation is the second-largest Indian tribe. It's also one of the poorest, with an average per capita yearly income of $13,346, according to the 2010 US Census.[44] Bealer's grandparents and parents worked hard to provide an opportunity for her to pursue a college degree.

In 2006, she graduated from Rice University with a degree in chemical and biomolecular engineering. She chose her field because of her commitment to serving her people. While it may have been more intuitive for Bealer to pursue a career as a social worker to advocate on behalf of her tribe, instead she took a job with Merck, a Fortune 100 pharmaceutical conglomerate.

"I came to work for a big pharmaceutical company because I felt like it would offer me the biggest platform to do something about health care disparities on a large scale for Native American populations," she shared.

Bealer could have studied medicine or founded a nonprofit health clinic. Though she considered returning to a reservation to teach, instead she felt drawn to big business, desiring not to earn a hefty salary or posh benefits, but to serve her people by addressing some of the root causes affecting Native Americans.

"The opportunity to reach the masses was with Merck," Bealer shared. "We have tens of thousands of employees and a distribution network across the globe."

She continued, "Merck presented a big opportunity to perhaps impact more people there than I would have if I had gone the nonprofit route or a smaller advocacy organization route. Those jobs may have been more rewarding—I may have felt the good on more of a daily basis than I do at Merck—but I think there's power in Merck's scale and scope."

At Merck, Bealer has the opportunity to serve the health needs of Native Americans directly by bringing health care solutions to these communities, and also by coleading a new job-creation venture: Project Sacred Dream.

Over the course of her seven years at Merck, Bealer has worked her way up the company ladder and now serves as associate director for global commercial assessment. Along the way, Merck has given her increasing opportunities to serve the community so close to her heart. For Merck, this is not just an act of goodwill. They know how crucial it is to provide meaningful work for their employees.

Their decision to provide Bealer with opportunities to serve Native American populations will bring her full abilities and enthusiasm to the table. Through her efforts, she has started to see a convergence of her heritage and her work.

This connection has at times been a source of tension for her. "I'm considered an 'urban Indian.' I live in a big city and have a mainstream job. There's a lot of guilt for me," Bealer confessed. "In working for a Fortune 100 company, I don't think I could do it if I didn't believe it was somehow helping my people."

But helping others is also good business. By providing lifesaving vaccines and medicines to Native American customers—as well as health care materials—Merck is breaking into a vastly under-served population. Expected to increase 33 percent by 2050, the Native American population is an emerging market.

Merck wants to position itself as a leader in this developing market. So Bealer recognized an opportunity to pitch a business plan that would help the Native American population—and Merck.

Last year she and her coworker Pam Abaza began dreaming about a new venture that would address health care disparities existing between the Native American population and other populations within the United States. For example, according to the Centers for Disease Control and Prevention's

National Center for Health Statistics, Native Americans have higher rates of heart disease and diabetes than any other population in the United States.[45]

Poverty often is the root of health problems for the Native American population. According to the National Center for Health Statistics, Native Americans have more unmet medical needs "due to cost of care" than any other population in the United States.[46]

Although their end goal was to address health care issues for the Native American population, Bealer and Abaza realized they also had to confront unemployment. While Bealer's passion for Native Americans comes from her heritage, Abaza's stemmed from the adoption of her daughter from a Lakota Tribe in South Dakota. Her daughter's Lakota birth mother was 15 years old when she became pregnant, and she lived in a one-room trailer with her family of 10.

Her Lakota grandmother named her granddaughter *Ta Woimbli Waste Win*, which means "her good dream woman" in Lakota. In her honor, the Merck project Bealer leads has been named Project Sacred Dream—a business plan for a 500-employee call center, owned by the tribe (managed by Merck subsidiary Telerx, a call center company), located on the Cheyenne River Sioux reservation in South Dakota.

With more than 10,000 residents and a 90 percent unemployment rate, Cheyenne River Sioux is desperate for a major job-creation initiative.

Because call centers have low startup costs, are not labor intensive, and do not require a workforce with advanced degrees, they are an ideal venture for this community. Bealer and Abaza have their sights and ambition firmly set on resolving many of the pervasive health issues disproportionately plaguing Native American populations, such as diabetes and heart disease.[47] But they realize jobs must come first.

"You can't talk to people living in extreme poverty about health care," she said. "Their day-to-day concerns are about how they are going to feed their families. They have no margin to talk about chronic health conditions. The number one thing we need to do in these communities is create jobs. That's the underlying issue beneath the health care problems."

Once they build their business, they'll fix their sights on supporting the local health clinics serving Cheyenne River Sioux. If it goes well, they hope to replicate this model in reservations across the country. In addition to employing 500 Cheyenne River Sioux workers, they believe their first call center will generate $80 million in revenues for the tribe over the next five years with a percentage (yet to be determined) allocated to Merck's subsidiary.

But Project Sacred Dream is not just benefiting the tribe. It's also creating inroads for Merck.

First, Project Sacred Dream helps Merck build bridges. For example, it is forging a unique partnership with Indian Health Services, the US Department of Health and Human Services agency that serves the Native American population. Second, Merck's partnership with the Native American population will help it meet requirements to join the Billion Dollar Roundtable, a group of corporations that each invest $1 billion in women-and minority-owned suppliers. Finally, the project is paving a pathway for the future. If successful, Project Sacred Dream will be a prototype Merck would replicate in other emerging markets. It is also a cost-effective plan, since Project Sacred Dream is an onshore call center at an offshore call center price (tax incentives and tax credits are included because of its reservation location). In sum, Project Sacred Dream aligns with Merck's current mission and future dreams.

While it would be idealistic to say narratives like Bealer's always occur, Project Sacred Dream isn't a fairytale. Bealer knew her company. She understood its values—the motivations driving Merck's leaders—and where it wanted to pitch stakes for future economic expansion.

Bealer also had a passion for helping her people. And because she positioned her goodwill in such a way that would also benefit her company, she could meet real needs.

When passionate and driven individuals like Bealer work hand in hand with corporations like Merck, good can be carried out on a large scale.

BIG, BAD BUSINESS

Consider these terms: *multinational corporations*, *big business*, *factories*.

For most of us, these terms conjure wholly negative reactions. Among the correlations they beckon for us are sweatshops, the 1 percent, boycotts, child labor, and Hollywood caricatures like Mr. Burns from *The Simpsons* or movie villains like the miserly Mr. Potter from the classic *It's a Wonderful Life*. And there are valid reasons for some of these correlations.

Upton Sinclair profiled vile working conditions in many American factories during the Industrial Revolution in his classic book *The Jungle*:

> All day long this man would toil thus . . . his whole being centered upon the purpose of making twenty-three instead of twenty-two and a half cents an hour; and then his product would be reckoned up by the census taker, and jubilant captains of industry would boast of it in their banquet halls, telling how our workers are nearly twice as efficient as those of any other country. If we are the greatest nation the sun ever shone upon, it would seem to be mainly because we have been able to goad our wage-earners to this pitch of frenzy.[48]

Sinclair described a grim reality for many American factory workers in the early 20th century. For them, work felt like a curse, not a gift. It was backbreaking, soul-squelching labor. Sadly, these same conditions aren't merely relegated to American history books. Across the globe, many factories still feature similarly deplorable conditions.

On April 24, 2013, a garment factory in Bangladesh collapsed, killing over 1,100 workers in the world's deadliest garment-industry accident. Substandard construction and poor management oversight caused the disaster.[49] The factory produced clothing for a number of leading European retailers, including discount clothier Primark.[50] The tragedy inflicted unspeakable pain on families throughout the country. The lasting devastation from this corporate negligence is hard to overstate.

Sinclair and the Bangladeshi disaster prompt uncomfortable questions. Are most big businesses squeezing every penny of profit out of poor workers?

The conventional portrayal of big business indicates that multinational corporations are part of the problem, not the solution. There is, of course, some validity to these claims. Some business owners do use disgraceful practices at the expense of their workers.

But there is much more to the story.

THE JOURNEY TO PROSPERITY

Benjamin Powell, professor of economics at Suffolk University, published a controversial article in 2008 titled, "In Defense of Sweatshops." In the article, he explained why he holds what might seem like a heartless position on this labor practice:

> Not only are sweatshops better than current worker alternatives, but they are also part of the process of development that ultimately raises living standards. . . . When companies open sweatshops, they bring technology and physical capital with them. Better technology and more capital raise worker productivity. Over time this raises their wages. As more sweatshops open, more alternatives are available to workers, raising the amount a firm must bid to hire them.[51]

In an article for *Forbes*, Powell notes that 4,500 sweatshops in Bangladesh employ more than four million workers. And "while 77 percent of Bangladeshis live on less than $2 a day—the international poverty standard—and 43 percent live on less than $1.25 a day, workers at the Bangladeshi 'sweatshops' average more than $2 a day."[52]

Examining the economic paths of the United States, Japan, South Korea, and Taiwan, Powell composes a case for why sweatshops are a necessary step in the economic development of a country. Poor countries often start with the conditions described in *The Jungle*, but over time, workers earn wages that lead to better education for them and their children. This leads to innovation and competition for profit making, which means new factories improve wages and working conditions for more people.

In no way is this to argue for the acceptance of appalling working environments. Rather, it is to shine light on the fact that the best way to overcome poor conditions is through market forces, which allow workers, owners, and advocates—not faraway bureaucrats—to get to work improving local conditions.

In recent years, we've witnessed this positive path across Asia. In 2012 alone, average factory wages in China escalated 14 percent. In manufacturing, specifically, worker wages have increased 71 percent since 2008. China has grown into a global business powerhouse over the past few decades because of its competent and increasingly educated workforce.[53] Factory workers also have experienced rising wages and improved factory conditions.

This is a proven path of economic development. As countries like Vietnam, Bangladesh, India, Malaysia, and China opened their borders to trade, big business flowed in. Job creation and increased provision of high-quality products and services has driven the dramatic decreases in extreme poverty we documented in Chapter Two.

RECAPTURING THE HEART OF BIG BUSINESS

In light of these overwhelming data, it would be easy to view awful working conditions as a necessary step toward prosperity. But the road to affluence need not be paved with tragedies like the one in Bangladesh in 2013.

"With freedom comes the possibility of gain from unethical behavior," writes Hunter Baker in the *Journal of Markets and Morality*. "That objection is undoubtedly true. There is little question that these bad acts have happened, are happening, and will happen . . . [but] competition allows for rapid natural reform because bad actors cannot hold their customer base."[54]

Baker goes on to celebrate competition as a means to counteract *The Jungle*, cautioning the critics of business to consider the alternatives:

> The critics of competition [like Sinclair] deplore what they perceive as the great waste of effort caused by human beings trying to excel [against] one another in the market. Cooperation, in their minds, is the answer. The problem with cooperation is that *cooperation for* can just as easily become *cooperation against*.

Governments with the loftiest goals have often become the enemies of their people. Power, once centralized with a noble purpose, is extraordinarily difficult to limit and disperse. Competition may not be optimal in the same way democracy probably underperforms government by a saintly king, but it is a decidedly lower risk proposition in a fallen world.[55]

Herein lies an unmatched opportunity for values-driven business leaders to outcompete, outsmart, and outmatch the scoundrels. Profits and worker vitality are not diametrically opposed. Great companies see their profits as an outcome of safe, healthy, productive, and happy employees. When John Mackey founded Whole Foods Market, he built his company to serve the farmers providing their products, the customers shopping in their stores, and the investors putting their money into his company. Profits have been a wonderful outcome, but not the sole motivator or mission of the business.

In *Built to Last*, author Jim Collins notes that top-tier global companies rarely discuss profits.[56] The companies Collins identifies—such as Ford, Marriott, and 3M—produce abundant profits, of course, but this is a byproduct of the way they conduct their business, not the end in and of itself. One of the companies Collins lauds as a visionary company is

Merck, Elyse Bealer's employer.

George Merck II, the founder of the Fortune 100 multinational corporation, understood that the vision for his business was to solve societal problems, not simply to increase shareholder value. "We try to remember that medicine is for the patient," he shared in 1950. "We try never to forget that medicine is for the people. It is not for the profits. The profits follow, and if we have remembered that, they have never failed to appear. The better we have remembered it, the larger they have been."[57]

Earlier in his life, he described his vision for his company as a "service to humanity."[58] It was that vision that drove Merck's workers to develop vaccines. Merck's vision is inscribed throughout Merck corporate buildings today. Because of George Merck's dream, entire diseases have been eradicated. And this same vision undergirds Elyse Bealer's efforts today.

What Merck understands is that companies focused on lasting success take into account a longer and broader view of human flourishing than do companies created to make a quick buck at the expense of their workers. Merck invests in its people and customers because its guiding vision transcends quarterly profit statements.

Companies like Enron and the Bangladeshi garment company might have momentary success, but it is shortsighted. "Succeeding" at the expense of your employees and customers will eventually lead to collapse. Such was the case for Enron. The companies that last—like Merck—understand their vision and purpose extends far beyond quarterly income statements.

BIG SMALL BUSINESSES

It's almost impossible to reconcile the Merck vision with our negative perceptions of big business. One reason is that many corporations have forgotten their purpose—or at least neglected to communicate it. This is what John Mackey, founder and CEO of Whole Foods, identifies as "the unintended consequence of low-consciousness of business."[59]

In 2007, Merck paid more than $4 billion to settle 27,000 lawsuits related to its painkilling drug Vioxx. In 2011, a Merck business unit was convicted of a misdemeanor for illegal marketing of Vioxx, shaking the company's very foundation. The company paid close to $1 billion in damages because of its infractions.[60]

Whether the Vioxx scandal was a purposeful Merck coverup or an honest mistake is still debated. But what is clear is that when large companies like Merck lose sight of their purpose, it's easy for them to become derailed.

"The pharmaceutical industry's drop in public esteem has been precipitous," wrote John Mackey.

"It used to be a greatly admired industry with a clear sense of higher purpose; companies invested heavily to develop miracle drugs that saved, improved and extended lives. . . . The industry's loss of purpose has coincided with its declining reputation and a major increase in ethical lapses."[61]

To its credit, Merck has admitted its wrongdoing and recently has made strides to invest in leaders like Bealer, thus reclaiming the mission of the company George Merck founded. Its leaders have placed confidence in the company's researchers who "try never to forget that medicine is for the people."[62]

Whether or not they will turn things around is still uncertain, but it will be possible only if Merck's leaders remember their history. Many business leaders have lost sight of their irreplaceable role in flourishing societies. They've forgotten the problems their founders built their companies to solve. In the Vioxx case, this much was clear.

Gallup reported that Americans' trust in big business declined from 45 percent in 1975 to 21 percent in 2013. Yet all the while, trust in small business remained remarkably high. Sixty-five percent placed confidence in the institution of small business.[63]

We all love a good rags-to-riches entrepreneur story. From the barbershop owner to the bold inventor like Henry Ford, these stories are quintessential

---

Nearly all of the big, faceless corporations documentary makers love to hate started as small businesses.

Americana. But do we love when these businesses become big? Or would we rather they simply stay small? Do we like when they start interacting with one another in the global marketplace?

Nearly all of the big, faceless corporations documentary makers love to hate started as small businesses. They all began local and expanded globally. From Merck to Ford Motor Company—they started as "mom and pop" small businesses. Many companies—some of which we'll feature later in this book—remain small. And that's certainly not a bad thing. There's something unique and personal about small and local businesses. But it's also not a bad thing if small companies grow big.

Big or small, the best global companies are anchored to their roots. They're smitten with their founders' stories and have not lost sight of their corporate *heart and soul*. Of course there are exceptions and homogenizing mergers and acquisitions, but those who have kept the founders' stories as their identity hold themselves to their core purpose and a high standard of excellence. In the "visionary companies" Jim Collins describes, leaders are acutely focused on building institutions that address the problems their companies were created to solve.

REMEMBERING THE MISSION

Because of the Vioxx scandal, expiring vaccine patents, and delays in rolling out new products caused by federal regulation, Merck's business has lagged over the past few years. In September 2013, Merck's leaders announced a three-year plan to lay off 20 percent of its 80,000-person global workforce. Bealer has retained her job. But often her work feels like toil, not the world-changing efforts she signed up for.

"It was really hard for me for a while to wrestle with whether I'm living up to my values by working in 'corporate America,'" Bealer confessed. "Especially for an industry like pharmaceuticals, where there's so much bad press and negative publicity."

There are many days she does not feel connected to George Merck II's grand vision. She's had friends who have been laid off, and many of her days feel laborious. She feels the pain of toiling within a slow-moving corporate behemoth.

Her experience is not unique for workers in big business around the world. More than that, it's not unusual for workers in any industry or job—non-profit or for-profit, big, small, or somewhere in between. As Christians, our everyday lives on the job must be theologically cogent if our theology is any good at all. As we stated in Chapter Two, we believe God created work to be an inherently *good* thing. But as a result of evil entering the story in the Garden of Eden, work lost its sheen. God's intent and purpose for work has become cloudy.

Workers in many garment factories around the world, and young professionals working at companies whose vision feels trite or soulless, feel only work's burdens. After their separation from God in Genesis, humans are told the consequences of sin will permeate their daily work: "Cursed is the ground because of you; through painful toil you will eat food from it all the days of your life" (Gen. 3:17b). Since that time, struggle has become a primary element of our existence. Every day can feel like near-purposeless labor.

Even for Bealer, there are days, and even whole weeks, where she feels primarily the clouds and gloom of work. Employees of massive corporations perhaps feel this dichotomy most severely. Because of the impersonal nature of large institutions, this tug between the redemptive and corrupting aspects of work is felt every day.

But then Bealer says she remembers her purpose. She walks into a meeting for Project Sacred Dream or completes a commercial assessment valuing a lifesaving oncology product, and she recalls Merck's vision. She reflects on the managers and senior Merck leaders who have invested so deeply in her. And she thinks about the Native American families being served by her company and those who will one day be able to provide for their families because of their jobs at the various call centers.

She thinks of *Ta Woimbli Waste Win*—her good dream woman—and families like hers who will experience a better future and healthier lives because of her work. When she recaptures the enduring vision driving her personal and corporate mission, Bealer remembers why she enlisted in big business. It was because Merck is one of the world's legendary health and wellness companies. And working with this company provided her the greatest opportunity to serve the populations she cares most about with much-needed pharmaceutical products, services, and jobs.

It's interesting to speculate where Bealer would be today if she had not worked for Merck. What if she had decided not to join the corporate world? No doubt, her love for her people would still drive her to serve. Most likely, she would be doing life-changing work. But would it have been to the same scale? The answer is likely no.

In the same vein, today is an age where young and talented individuals are seeking to change the world—to find solutions to real-world needs like poverty, the water crisis, or health care disparities. What if many more like-minded individuals would be pioneers like Bealer—individuals with a desire to change the world for good and on a large scale? Imagine the vast platform for good that could be created when individuals bent on seeing change partner with the corporate world.

5

**ENTREPRENEURSHIP
AT THE GRASSROOTS**

Create–sell–invest–give: this is the consistent cycle of any flourishing entrepreneur. And when entrepreneurs flourish, people and places flourish.

These principles translate into every language and context, from the grassroots level to looming skyscrapers, from Manhattan to Malawi. This cycle led Adrian Groff to join his family's business and Henry Kaestner to invest in emerging small businesses around the globe. This same cycle fueled George Merck's passion to solve our world's most-pressing health problems and diseases.

On the business spectrum, some entrepreneurs are working at the very edge of commerce. Grassroots entrepreneurs develop businesses in places established businesses are unwilling or unable to go.[64] Some of these enterprises might grow or evolve into small or medium-sized businesses. But most of the businesses in this category operate on the margins of markets.

Some have been called *social enterprises*. This label attempts to categorize these enterprises by their commitment to the social challenges they preeminently aim to solve. It recognizes the risks the enterprises take by operating in places where the market is not yet fully functioning. In general, social enterprises are known for elevating people and purpose over profits. Social entrepreneurs are motivated "primarily by social benefit."[65]

William Drayton, CEO of Ashoka, describes it this way:

> The job of a social entrepreneur is to recognize when a part of society is stuck and to provide new ways to get it unstuck. He or she finds what is not working and solves the problem by changing the system, spreading the solution and persuading entire societies to take new leaps. Social entrepreneurs are not content just to give a fish or teach how to fish. They will not rest until they have revolutionized the fishing industry.[66]

Yet, as we've argued, human flourishing is the heart and soul of entrepreneurship in general. Inadvertently, the label of social entrepreneurship can create a false paradigm—that enterprise is inherently *unsocial*. It suggests that companies like Merck, Groff's, and Whole Foods are somehow socially second-rate enterprises.

We believe it's unhelpful to categorize the organizations we'll feature in this chapter as *social enterprises*. They're certainly social, but so are the other companies we've profiled. In this chapter, we're looking at enterprises operating at the margins of the global markets.

These enterprises operating at the margins reach

Create–sell–invest–give: this is the consistent cycle
of any flourishing entrepreneur.

---

the impoverished among even developed countries,
but they tend to focus primarily on the developing
world. In the developing world, the need for such
services is greater. For example, more than 50 percent of the gross domestic product in sub-Saharan
Africa is derived not from traditional business, but
through the informal sector—street markets, subsis-
tence farms, household vendors, and others.[67] If we
care about reducing poverty, we have to think cre-
atively and look at innovative solutions found outside the formal economy.

RISING TIDE

In the lives of the entrepreneurs we meet, we
see glimpses of a much bigger story unfolding—
entrepreneurship is allowing families and communities to flourish. Alex Forrester is clean-cut, wears
a suit, and has a Harvard degree. But his hero was
born on the other side of the world. "You've never
heard of her," he said at a recent gathering of entrepreneurs. "But she changed my life."[68]

Genet Demmellash is from Ethiopia. When the

country's dictator turned his military against his own citizens, she not only lost her brother and sister, but also was separated from her two-year-old daughter. In a refugee camp in the early 1980s, she finally had the chance to receive a visa to enter the United States—where she vowed she'd one day reunite with her daughter.

Working extra shifts as a waitress in the United States, she began to realize she would never be able to pay for her daughter's flight on her current salary. So she took to what she knew: sewing. Working as a seamstress late in the evenings, she created beautiful dresses and gowns that became highly sought after by friends and then by the larger community.

She used her skills to provide a valuable service to her community. And it was the income from this business that enabled her daughter, Alfa, to come home. It was this daughter whom Forrester met as an underclassman at Harvard.

"The daughter is the girl I met in college and fell in love with," he said. "Inspired by Genet's story, we founded Rising Tide Capital, and a few years later we got married."[69]

Alfa Demmellash was able to attend Harvard University because of God's graciousness and her mom's love and thriving sewing business. Today, Alex Forrester and Alfa Demmellash provide tools to give those like Genet a chance to break out of intergenerational poverty.

They take risks on clients most American banks might dismiss. Many of their clients have families and work full time but make less than $33,000 a year in the suburbs of New York City, where making $48,000 annually is the baseline for sustainability.[70] Overlooked, these individuals often use their skills to start businesses to supplement their income.[71]

Many individuals are simply unaware of the resources and tools available to them. That's where Rising Tide steps in. Rising Tide acts as a first rung on the entrepreneurial ladder, helping these riskier and more vulnerable individuals move beyond mere survival. More than 90 percent are minorities, and 80 percent of program constituents have low to moderate incomes. Though nearly half have a college degree, 29 percent are unemployed at the start of the program, and 68 percent are women.[72]

Coming alongside these entrepreneurs, Rising Tide Capital provides a 12-week business training program, as well as coaching and a connection to a network of microfinance providers—those willing to provide small loans to business owners.

Established in 2006, Rising Tide Capital has now helped 300 graduates get their businesses up and running, with another 283 businesses in progress. Since its founding, Rising Tide has served significant numbers of grassroots entrepreneurs, growing at an average pace of 41 percent annually.[73]

On average, a new business bankrolled by Rising Tide Capital opens every 12 days.[74]

In addition to helping individual entrepreneurs, Rising Tide's model benefits its local communities. As these individuals expand their businesses, they are hiring others, which creates jobs.

"We believe that one of the most important tools to fight against poverty is the entrepreneurial energy that already exists in every community," said Forrester.

Ultimately, though, it's about the individual. Today, Forrester and Demmellash have a baby boy, Noah. Because of his grandmother's sacrifice, Noah now has opportunities Genet would never have dreamed of. Through entrepreneurship, Noah and children like him are being freed from intergenerational poverty.

By leveraging donation capital, Forrester is able to extend the boundaries of the markets, unleashing the creativity and gifts of entrepreneurs slipping through the cracks. The capital and approach Forrester uses is different from that of his for-profit peers. He leverages a model called "patient capital" from Jacqueline Novogratz, founder and CEO of Acumen Fund, one of the world's largest venture capital funds investing in social enterprises.[75] The entrepreneurs Novogratz and Forrester invest in "have difficulty getting money from traditional venture capital firms," creating market opportunities for nonprofit investors like Rising Tide and Acumen to step in.

Rising Tide has had success working with entrepreneurs within US borders. Other investors, like Novogratz, are deploying a similar training and investment strategy to unlock the potential of grassroots entrepreneurs beyond the US.

GRASSROOTS BANGLADESHI ENTREPRENEURS

In the 1970s, Muhammad Yunus, an economics professor from Bangladesh, began supporting vulnerable communities throughout his country. While heading the Rural Economics Program at the University of Chittagong, he frequented markets across Bangladesh. He met poor women who were leading very small businesses. Over time, he learned that if they had an initial investment in their grassroots businesses, their profits would increase dramatically.

Yunus created Grameen Bank out of his desire to ensure entrepreneurs had access to small loans to invest in small-business opportunities. Instead of requiring physical collateral, he used a group guarantee, allowing these women to be the collateral for one another. These small-business owners proved to be a great investment. Defying expectation, they repaid their loans on time. And the modern microfinance movement was born.

Yunus's innovation underscored the heart of entrepreneurship. It affirmed the gifts and abilities of the people in his materially poor communities. It recognized that though these women had very limited financial resources, they could solve problems.

What originated from a graduate school in Bangladesh has grown into a global phenomenon. In 2006, Yunus received the Nobel Peace Prize for his innovation. Today, microfinance programs provide small loans, business training, and savings accounts to more than 100 million grassroots entrepreneurs around the world.[76]

In Ecuador, a study by Gary Woller and Robert Parsons of Brigham Young University found that "the benefits of microfinance programs are economic as well as social . . . [and] the economic benefits of microfinance programs extend beyond program beneficiaries into the wider local community."[77]

We are microfinance practitioners and have seen firsthand the power of unleashing entrepreneurship in the developing world. When done with the love of Jesus, helping hardworking men and women start or expand a business breaks the cycles of physical and spiritual poverty.

However, microfinance is no panacea for global poverty. It is a way of delivering financial services to those excluded from the formal financial sector.

But just as payday and subprime mortgage lending in our country can create more problems than they solve, microfinance can actually further entrap families in unhealthy debt.

In 2009, this reality became headline news when evidence surfaced that several commercial microfinanciers in Andhra Pradesh, India, were pressuring poor Indian entrepreneurs into taking larger loans than they were capable of repaying. These predatory microlenders deployed aggressive debt-collection practices, and tragically, several of these borrowers committed suicide because of their extreme debt.[78]

Increasingly, leaders in the microfinance movement have recognized the need to provide more than just appropriately priced business loans. These leaders have rallied together to create standards for best practice, such as the Pro-Poor Seal of Excellence and the Smart Campaign, both of which aim to remind the microfinance movement of its roots.

As such, the movement has expanded to include savings services, financial literacy and vocational training, and insurance. The Ministry of the Family in Nicaragua did a pilot study to investigate whether capital or the combination of capital and vocational training provides a better safety net against the effects of natural disaster—for example, the droughts that are common in this region, destroying harvests and devastating the lives of rural farmers.[79] (See figure 3.)

FIGURE 3. EFFECT OF VOCATIONAL TRAINING ON COMMUNITIES SUFFERING FROM DROUGHT

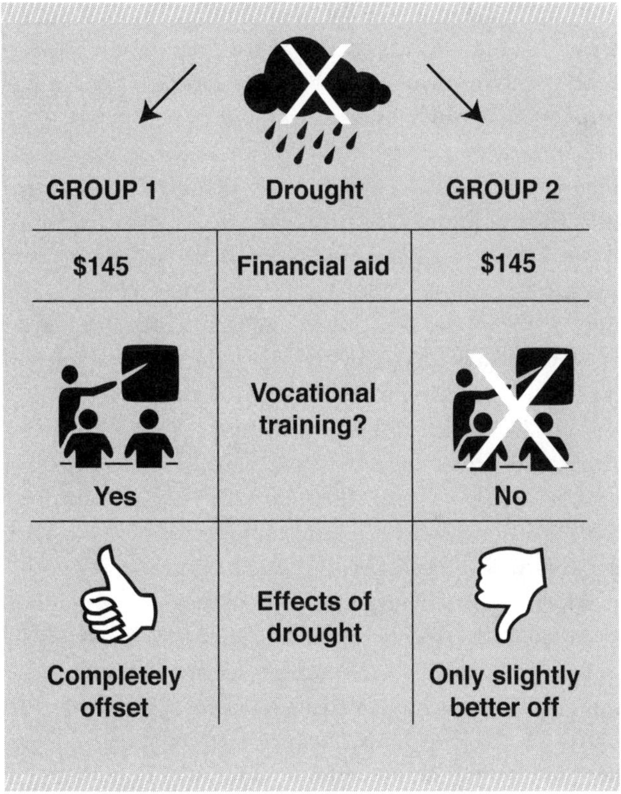

GROUP 1	Drought	GROUP 2
$145	Financial aid	$145
Yes	Vocational training?	No
Completely offset	Effects of drought	Only slightly better off

Source: Ministry of the Family (Nicaragua) pilot study.

One group received $145. A second received $145, plus vocational training. Though the first group was better off than it had been without the money, the second group was assisted dramatically: "For total and food consumption, as well as for income, the negative impact of [drought] shocks was completely offset."[80]

Individuals receiving business training used their recently acquired employment skills to find other jobs to supplement their income during the drought. Basic business skills, alongside increased economic advantage, can serve as a crucial and effective safety net for the poor. It's true in the lives of the American entrepreneurs served by Rising Tide, and it's true in far-off places like Bangladesh and Rwanda.

In the Middle Ages, *montes pietatius* were charities similar to urban food banks, created as an alternative to loan sharks. These charities provided low-interest loans to poor families. Started by Franciscans, they became widespread throughout Europe.

Even Pope Julius II gave an edict endorsing *montes pietatius*. In folklore, Saint Nicholas generously provided a poor man dowries for his three daughters, gold coins in three purses. The symbol of gold coins in three purses became the symbol of pawn shops and fit with his title of patron saint.

In the 1300s, people in poverty met caring friars when they entered the doors of pawn shops. The shops existed to help the poor get back on their feet, and these friars had their best interests in mind. Today, often the opposite is true. Over time, pawn shop owners lost sight of their identity. Created for good, pawn shops have drifted away from their purpose—instead of caring for the needy, they have become an instrument to often prey on individuals or families in distress.

Modern-day social entrepreneurs should hold the story of pawn shops closely. It is easy for entrepreneurs to lose sight of the problems they seek to solve and the mission they set out to accomplish.

OUR RWANDAN HEROES

When I (Peter) arrived in Rwanda five years after the genocide, the nation was still in mourning.

In 1994, radicals from Rwanda's ethnic majority sought to eradicate the ethnic minority. For years, fanatics had been stirring national animosity toward the minority. When the president, Juvénal Habyarimana, was killed when his plane was shot down, the radicals instigated ethnic cleansing. During the genocide, more than 800,000 people were murdered.[81]

How would you even begin rebuilding your family, let alone your nation, after such societal devastation? My friend Marie Jeanne Uwimana didn't have the luxury of pondering that question. Uwimana and her two sons were the only three in her family of 70 to survive.

After sharing her story with a widow in her neighborhood, she realized that her Rwandan neighbors—whether victims or perpetrators in the genocide—were destitute and in need of help. She and 19 other women, both ethnic majority and minority, decided to meet weekly for prayer and encouragement. Eagerly desiring a new identity, they gave themselves a name—*Inkingi*, translated: "pillar."

Their goal was simple: to support one another and find some way to provide for their families. As they started meeting, in addition to praying together, they also agreed to save $0.20 a week. What may seem like an inconsequential amount began the process of creating a small-business empire.

With the accumulated savings, they first invested in one of the members—a woman who had just been released from jail because of her role in the genocide. They determined she had the greatest need. With just over $2.00, she purchased charcoal and began selling it in her neighborhood.

After six months, they began increasing their monthly savings to $1.72 per member. Again, they took the accumulated savings and would invest it in whichever member had the best business opportunity or an emergency. Two years later, they were saving $3.00 per month per woman.

And then they turned the corner. With larger capital investments, they were able to earn more and save more. By 2003, they purchased two grinding machines that enabled them to deliver processed maize flour to area schools, collectively saving a staggering $28,000.

Ten years after they first started meeting, they invested $20,000 to buy a truck to transport their product to schools across Rwanda. Through their business, all 20 women paid for their children to graduate from university; the one adult child who did not go to university is the truck driver for the business.

When I visited Rwanda a few months ago, I got to see this truck and hear how proud they were of the impact of their group. They are now moving into real estate and are looking to build 20 modern houses in the same neighborhood over the next few years.

Proudly, they gave me a tour of the church they were building and shared about the widows and other community members they've been able to serve. Their collective average income per month from the group's productive assets is $600. Their bank balance is now more than $45,000.

And it all started with $0.20 apiece.

This is the power of savings, patient capital, hard work, and community solidarity. Our organization, HOPE International, serves entrepreneurs as a nonprofit. And organizations like HOPE have a role to play in promoting entrepreneurship.

But the possibilities extend far beyond just

for-profit and nonprofit ventures. Carter Crock-ett, the inaugural director for the Center for Entre-preneurial Leadership at Gordon College, recently shared, "These are exciting times. Never before have so many people had so many options for addressing challenges around the globe." Crockett believes the explosion of business models and legal statuses to choose from—business, nonprofit, L3C, B-Corp, and so forth—demonstrates the wide range of ave-nues. More important than legal status, however, is a commitment to holding fast to the mission of the organization as it grows. Only then will our enter-prises avoid the fate of pawn shops and continue to meet valuable needs in our communities.

ENTREPRENEURSHIP ON THE FRONT LINES

The tables at Purple Door Coffee in Denver fill up early with regulars. On the surface, it looks like a typ-ical urban, upscale coffee shop—complete with fash-ionably upholstered chairs, a hardwood coffee bar, a chalkboard menu, and exposed brick walls opening to full-length windows with views of the city.

And it is a regular coffee shop—except that it's employing homeless youth.

Madison Chandler, cofounder of Purple Door Coffee, was formerly an intern with an organization serving homeless youth in Denver. While there, she and another intern, Mark Smesrud, realized they had a mutual love for coffee and a passion to see Denver homeless youth get off the streets.

She and Smesrud created a space that merged their love of coffee and their desire to meet one of greatest obstacles facing the homeless in Denver— lack of employment. Chandler and Smesrud recognized a problem in their community and identified entrepreneurship as the perfect solution. They also knew the Five Points neighborhood in Northeast Denver was devoid of a great coffee shop.

Today, Purple Door has become a fixture at the corner of Welton and 30th Streets. It's a neighborhood meeting spot and a purveyor of fine coffee. Chandler and Smesrud are helping formerly homeless youth gradually recover their worth and become prepared for other full-time work. They epitomize the best of the social entrepreneurship movement. They lead a profitable business but employ individuals often overlooked by their commercial competitors. At the margins of the markets, they serve coffee at a beautiful nexus of commerce and charity.

THE SOUL OF ENTREPRENEURSHIP

We believe in entrepreneurship. But it's more than just a belief. Again and again, as we've outlined in this book, human flourishing is not possible without robust entrepreneurship. When communities and countries lack enterprise, poverty surges.

Entrepreneurship creates the opportunities for people
to experience what it means to be truly human.

Entrepreneurship creates the opportunities for
people to experience what it means to be truly human.
It's part of our design to work and to experience what
Arthur Brooks has defined as "earned success"—the
fulfillment and joy that come when success is achieved
through hard work and grit.[82]

Brooks also acknowledges something else at the
heart of American entrepreneurship.[83] At our best,
we recognize success should not simply fuel hedo-
nism. "To pursue the happiness within our reach,
we do best to pour ourselves into faith, family, community and meaningful work," he wrote in the *New
York Times*.[84]

Meaningful work and financial success alone will
never produce human flourishing. As Brooks has
noted from his research, we need a broader understanding of human flourishing, one that emphasizes
the importance of faith, family, and community
as well. This is what social entrepreneurs like Alex
Forrester, Madison Chandler, and Mark Smesrud
understand. And these are the values ommercial
entrepreneurs like Adrian Groff, John Mackey,

and Henry Kaestner hold closely. A fuller vision of human flourishing thinks beyond personal gain, recognizing that entrepreneurship is a means by which people and places can thrive.

6

NOT JUST BUILDING
BIGGER BARNS

In the Genesis account of creation, we read: "Then the Lord God formed a man from the dust of the ground and breathed into his nostrils the breath of life, and the man became a living being" (Gen. 2:7).

Made in the image of God, the *imago dei,* humankind still bears the Creator's fingerprints. When a mother gives birth or we create something with our hands, we mirror the wonder of creation. In some small but significant way, we have the privilege of being cocreators with God. If we look closely enough, we see this ability to cocreate all around us as: an artist transforms a blank canvas into a masterpiece; a builder assembles planks and raw materials into the structure of a home; a pharmacist synthesizes substances that heal; or a farmer reaches down into the dirt, plants seeds, and watches life spring forth.

In *Three Magic Seeds,* the Acton Foundation for Entrepreneurial Excellence summarizes the creative process in this way: "To take the raw materials of nature, add time, talent and energy to make something valuable, or at least valuable to its owner. . . . This is about as close as you will come to the awesome experience of being a co-Creator."[85]

When God breathed into us *ruach,* the "breath of life" in Hebrew, we received an ability to create. But we know that creating merely to build bigger barns (Luke 12:18) will not bring people true happiness and ultimate meaning.

Meaning is not found through job creation or success alone, but through a lifelong commitment to faith, community, family, and meaningful work.

TRUE HAPPINESS

The March 12, 2012 *Time* cover story highlights 10 provocative ideas that are "changing your life." The seventh entry opened with the question, "What if the good life isn't really . . . all that good?" It went on to ask, "What if the very things so many of us strive for—a high-paying, powerful job; a beautiful house; a wardrobe of nice clothes in desirably small sizes; and a fancy education for our children to prep them for carrying on this way of life—turn out to be more trouble than they're worth?"[86]

Through research, the authors discovered that once you reach a threshold of wealth, the advantages diminish: "Research indicates that as you near the top, life stress increases so dramatically that its toxic effects essentially cancel out many positive aspects of succeeding."

In essence, they discovered what King Solomon, one of the richest and most successful men in the history of the world, wrote about in his memoir, Ecclesiastes, "Whoever loves money never has money enough; whoever loves wealth is never satisfied with his income" (Ecc. 5:10).[87]

Essentially Solomon is saying, "Money alone doesn't buy happiness." We were created for more.

BEYOND CREATION

In creating, we mirror the *imago dei*. Also central to the Christian faith is a lifestyle of generosity. We see this modeled by our Creator: "God so loved the world that he *gave*" (John 3:16). The story centers on the gift of Jesus, the gift of faith, and the gift of new life. In essence, our entire worldview hinges on a God who sacrifices himself for the good of others, for the sake of humanity. The God of Scripture is an extravagant philanthropist.

Jesus also famously said that it is "more blessed to give than to receive" (Acts 20:35), and science has repeatedly proven these ancient biblical words.

Elizabeth Dunn and Michael Norton, professors at the University of British Columbia and Harvard Business School, respectively, recently completed a study on happiness in countries such as Uganda and India.[88]

In that study, they gave each participant money—sometimes as little as $5. Half the participants were invited to buy gifts for themselves. The other half were invited to spend their money on someone else. At the end of the day, the participants reported their happiness levels.

Those who spent money on themselves remained the same as before. But those who gave—even in this simple exercise—were significantly happier than they were previously.

In fact, money may buy happiness, if it is linked to charity, argues Arthur Brooks in *Who Really Cares: The Surprising Truth about Compassionate Conservatism.* Those who donate to nonprofits are "43 percent more likely to say they are 'very happy'" than nongivers; nongivers are three and a half times more likely than givers to say they are "not happy at all," according to a study done by the University of Chicago.[89]

"Charitable giving . . . not only gives people the power to help others but also makes their lives meaningful," writes Brooks. "It also gives them the expressive power to support causes they care about—power the political system cannot provide—and ties them to others who have similar interests and passions."[90]

The University of Oregon carried out a study where students had the opportunity to give to a local food bank or add to their personal savings. When their brains were scanned, the individuals' reward centers were shown to activate most not when they *received*, but rather when they *gave*.[91]

A similar study in 2009 by Harvard Business School researchers discovered that giving produces a literal high. For those who give, the brain reacts a bit like it does for those who take cocaine or see a beautiful person or an art piece.[92]

When we give to others, the part of the brain that activates when receiving "rewarding stimuli"—the ventral striatum—also fires. In short, *we are hardwired to give.*

One of the world's wealthiest couples discovered this in a slum in India. At the 2012 National Prayer Breakfast in Washington, DC, Ravij Shah, administrator of USAID, commented that he had recently traveled with Bill and Melinda Gates to Bangalore, India.[93] What surprised him was that after they spent several days trying to figure out how to help those in poverty, Bill and Melinda stated time and again that they had never been happier.

Imagine, the couple who could afford literally anything they desired discovered their greatest joy came from using their wealth and their finances to help others. Why? As most individuals intuitively know, giving and serving are crucial elements of human flourishing.

Students interested in becoming entrepreneurs or businesspeople should pay special attention to this. It's no secret that there is money to be made in business: Bill Gates, George Merck, Henry Ford, and millions of workers that they employed have experienced some level of financial prosperity. But the happiest of these have discovered the joy that comes not from accumulating and amassing, but from giving and serving.

CELEBRITY ENDORSEMENT

Brad Pitt—yes, *that* Brad Pitt—reminds us that there is one more critical piece of true flourishing and living as individuals created in the *imago dei*. In an interview with *Rolling Stone*, Pitt shared about how his massive success left him longing for more:

> The emphasis now is on success and personal gain. [*Smiles*] I'm sitting in it, and I'm telling you, that's not it. . . . I'm the guy who's got everything. I know. But I'm telling you, once you've got everything, then you're just left with yourself. I've said it before and I'll say it again: it doesn't help you sleep any better, and you don't wake up any better because of it. Now, no one's going to want to hear that. I understand it. I'm sorry I'm the guy who's got to say it. But I'm telling you.[94]

Pitt knows that prosperity and success aren't sufficient to fulfill our deepest needs and longings. Even if we achieve astronomic levels of wealth and success, we can still be empty. We were created for more.

In his book *The Treasure Principle*, Randy Alcorn keeps a running list of quotes from some of the wealthiest—and unhappiest—modern men:

> "The care of $200 million is enough to kill anyone. There is no pleasure in it."
> —*W.H. Vanderbilt, railroad and shipping magnate*

> "I am the most miserable man on earth."
> —*John Jacob Astor, fur broker and America's original multimillionaire*

> "I have made many millions, but they have brought me no happiness."
> —*John D. Rockefeller, philanthropist and oil industrialist*

> "Millionaires seldom smile."
> —*Andrew Carnegie, philanthropist and steel tycoon*

Meaning is not found through job creation or success alone, but through a lifelong commitment to faith, community, family, and meaningful work.[95]

Ultimately, we are mirroring our Creator when we discover and demonstrate a desire to create and to give.

7

CONCLUSION

According to MIT economist Esther Duflo, hope is the fundamental element in reducing poverty.[96] Though it is difficult to quantify, hope's role in alleviating poverty is common sense.

Hope springs from having opportunity—a vision for the future. When individuals can see beyond their day-to-day needs to invest in tomorrow, they take risks. When students can recognize ideas are validated, they are free to experiment and push boundaries. And when parents can dream, they are more apt to save for their children's education, prompting multigenerational impact.

Around the globe, entrepreneurship and job creation are giving people hope—creating opportunity for individuals to invest in their dreams and the products and goods that societies need to flourish. In the process, more people are being lifted out of poverty than ever before. Since 1981, the percentage of people living in extreme poverty has plummeted.[97] In concert with the free market and globalization, private enterprise is the primary driver behind the fastest rate of poverty reduction in the world's history.[98]

From the diverse examples noted in this short book, we hope you see that what seems normal is in fact extraordinary. We pray you are encouraged to view entrepreneurship as an outflow of being made in the image of a creative God.

We hope that current and future generations learn to bridge the unhelpful chasm between the work of nonprofit activists and the work of business-people. It's time to erase the lines between a "noble nonprofit" and an "ordinary business." All work is infused with meaning. Entrepreneurs who pursue their God-given potential—and in time employ others on the basis of creative ideas that fulfill human needs—are undertaking incredibly noble work.

We hope you realize that it is a false divide to separate "impact investing" from the potential impact of investing in entrepreneurs who help build companies, provide employment, and bring hope to communities.

In businesses of all sizes and sectors, entrepreneurship that restores dignity and breaks the chains of poverty is experiencing a resurgence. With little fanfare, it is unleashing human potential and awakening men and women to truly live. And, yes, the engine of entrepreneurship and economic growth is raising resources to be given in support of other important nonprofit work where the free market is unable to reach.

Activism and business both play key roles in true flourishing. They complement each other. Our goal is for business students and professionals to discover the ways their skills, ingenuity, and hard work can help their communities reach their full potential.

Consider once more the example of John Mackey. When he launched Whole Foods Market, Mackey had no idea it would grow into one of the world's largest grocers. The former hippie never imagined he would become the CEO of a global for-profit company. But over the course of his professional journey, he realized he had been given a clear purpose to fulfill.

"Most of us earn our livelihood and provide for our families by working for companies, and all of us purchase the goods and services companies produce with extraordinary efficiency and ingenuity. The quality of our lives, our health, our overall well-being, and even our happiness depend greatly on the ways in which businesses operate," wrote Mackey. "Business is fundamentally about people working together cooperatively to create value for other people."[99]

We don't believe God has wired any of us accidentally. None of us should want Mackey to close Whole Foods Market and create a nonprofit food co-op. We wouldn't encourage Elyse Bealer to quit Merck to teach science to Native American students or tell Adrian Groff to work for the local shelter. It's not because those alternatives aren't meaningful or valid—they are. But our unique gifts are entrusted to us for a reason.

Small or big, operating across borders or at the margins, business is a sacred calling. So get to work.

Use your many talents and gifts to fuel businesses and organizations.

As you do, you'll see people and communities flourish.

ENDNOTES

1. Michael Novak, "For Catholics, the Vocation of Business Is the Main Hope for the World's Poor," *Forbes*, March 4, 2012, www.forbes.com/sites/realspin/2014/03/04/for-catholics-the-vocation-of-business-is-the-main-hope-for-the-worlds-poor/.

2. Klaus Issler, "Examining Jesus' Inclusion of Work Roles in His Parables," Institute for Faith, Work, and Economics, 2014, http://ifwe.s3.amazonaws.com/wp-content/uploads/2014/05/Jesus-and-the-Parables1.pdf.

3. Wayne Grudem and Barry Asmus, *The Poverty of Nations: A Sustainable Solution* (Wheaton, IL: Crossway, 2013), 270.

4. Hugh Whelchel, "What Is Flourishing?" Institute for Faith, Work, & Economics, May 20, 2013, www.blog.tifwe.org/what-is-flourishing.

5. Bryant L. Myers, *Walking with the Poor: Principles and Practices of Transformational Development* (Maryknoll, NY: Orbis Books, 2011), 97.

6. Michael Novak, "The Joy of Capitalism: An Evening with Michael Novak" (event, American Enterprise Institute, Washington, DC, September 27, 2012), www.aei.org/events/2012/09/27/the-joy-of-capitalism-an-evening-with-michael-novak/.

7. Richard Florida, "Why Are Some Cities Happier Than Others?" *Atlantic*, March 22, 2011, www.theatlantic.com/business/archive/2011/03/why-are-some-cities-happier-than-others/72801/.

8. John Mackey and Raj Sisodia, *Conscious Capitalism: Liberating the Heroic Spirit of Business* (Boston: Harvard Business School Publishing Company, 2013), 12–13.

9. Erich Weede, "The Diffusion of Prosperity and Peace by

Globalization," *Independent Review* 9, no. 2 (2004), www.independent .org/pdf/tir/tir_09_2_1_weede.pdf.

10. Arthur Brooks, *The Road to Freedom* (Philadelphia: Basic Books, 2012), 74.

11. Nicholas Eberstadt, "What Is Wrong with the North Korean Economy," Caijing, July 1, 2011, www.aei.org/article/foreign-and-defense-policy/regional/asia/what-is-wrong-with-the-north-korean-economy/.

12. Jim Clifton, "The Coming Jobs War: What Every Leader Must Know about the Future of Job Creation," Gallup, October 4, 2011, www.gallup.com/press/150389/coming-jobs-war.aspx.

13. Alize Ferrarri, "Burden of Depressive Disorders by Country, Sex, Age, and Year: Findings from the Global Burden of Disease Study 2010," *PLOS Medicine* 10, no. 11 (2013), www. plosmedicine.org/article/info%3Adoi%2F10.1371%2Fjournal. pmed.1001547.

14. Seattle Pacific University, "About Dr. John Perkins," www. spu.edu/depts/perkins/john-perkins/index.asp.

15. Gallup, *State of the American Workplace: Employee Engagement Insights for U.S. Business Leaders*, 2013, www.gallup.com/strategicconsulting/ 163007/state-american-workplace.aspx.

16. Arthur Brooks, "A Formula for Happiness," *New York Times*, December 15, 2013.

17. Paul Rubin, "How to Roll Back the Demonizing of Free Markets," *Wall Street Journal*, December 25, 2013.

18. Mackey and Sisodia, *Conscious Capitalism*, 20.

19. Ibid., 3.

20. Ibid., 2.

21. Ibid., 3–4.

22. Dorothy Sayers, "Why Work?" in *Letters to a Diminished Church* (Nashville, TN: Thomas Nelson, 2004), http://centerforfaithandwork.com/sites/default/files/Sayers%20Why%20Work.pdf.

23. Dorothy Sayers, *Creed or Chaos?* (Manchester, NH: Sophia Institute Press, 1974), 89.

24. "U2's Bono Speaks at GU Global Social Enterprise Event," Vimeo video, 1:00, from a Georgetown University Global Social Enterprise event on November 12, 2012, posted by "Values & Capitalism," www.vimeo.com/53945169.

25. Laurence Chandy and Geoffrey Gertz, "With Little Notice, Globalization Reduced Poverty," YaleGlobal, July 5, 2011, http://yaleglobal.yale.edu/content/little-notice-globalization-reduced-poverty.

26. "Towards the End of Poverty," *Economist,* June 1, 2013, www.economist.com/news/leaders/21578665-nearly-1-billion-people-have-been-taken-out-extreme-poverty-20-years-world-should-aim.

27. But, you may be asking, what about those who are too ill to work? We don't want to negate the very real need for organizations like Mother Teresa's Missionaries of Charity that are specifically helping those unable to provide for themselves. Some organizations are needed to provide relief. Ultimately, though, job creation leads to healthier societies: job creation stimulates economic growth, and as a result, health care also progresses over time.

28. Mackey and Sisodia, *Conscious Capitalism*, 12–13.

29. Unless otherwise cited, all quotations are from personal interviews with the authors conducted between October 7 and October 30, 2013.

30. Gallup, "Confidence in Institutions, 2013," June 1–4, 2013, www.gallup.com/poll/1597/confidence-institutions.aspx.

31. Asim Khwaja, "The Missing Middle," Center for International Development, Harvard University, www.hks.harvard.edu/centers/cid/programs/entrepreneurial-finance-lab-research-initiative/the-missing-middle.

32. Major L. Clark III and Radwan N. Saade, "The Role of Small Business in Economic Development of the United States: From the End of the Korean War (1953) to the Present" (working paper, US Small Business Administration, Washington, DC, September 2010), www.sba.gov/advocacy/7540/12143.

33. Arthur Brooks, *Social Entrepreneurship*, 1st ed. (Upper Saddle River, NJ: Prentice Hall Professional: 2008).

34. Gebremeskel H. Gebremariam, Tesfa G. Gebremedhin, and Randall W. Jackson, "The Role of Small Business in Economic Growth and Poverty Alleviation in West Virginia: An Empirical Analysis" (paper presented at American Agricultural Economics Association, Denver, CO, August 2004), 4–5, www.rri.wvu.edu/wp-content/uploads/2012/11/gebremedhinwp2004-10.pdf.

35. Ibid., 19.

36. Michael Novak, *The Spirit of Democratic Capitalism* (Lanham, MD: Madison Books, 1982), 13.

37. Stephen Slivinski, *Increasing Entrepreneurship Is a Key to Lowering Poverty Rates* (Phoenix, AZ: Goldwater Institute, November 13, 2012), www.goldwaterinstitute.org/sites/default/files/PR254%20

Increasing%20Entrepreneurship.pdf.

38. Doing Business, *About* Doing Business: *Measuring for Impact* (Washington, DC: World Bank, October 23, 2012), www.doingbusiness.org/~/media/GIAWB/Doing%20Business/Documents/Annual-Reports/English/DB13-Chapters/About-Doing-Business.pdf.

39. Ibid.

40. Khwaja, "The Missing Middle."

41. Bandwidth, "History," www.bandwidth.com/about-us/history.

42. Rob Moll and Rudy Carrasco, "Christian Investors Get Patient with Their Capital," *Forbes*, November 18, 2012, www.forbes.com/sites/realspin/2012/11/18/christian-investors-get-patient-with-their-capital/.

43. Public Broadcasting Service, "Trail of Tears," www.pbs.org/indiancountry/history/trail.html.

44. James McGirk, "The State of the Cherokee Nation: A Tale of Two Chiefs," *Time*, March 11, 2013, http://nation.time.com/2013/03/11/the-state-of-the-cherokee-nation-a-tale-of-two-chiefs/.

45. US Department of Health and Human Services, Centers for Disease Control and Prevention, "National Health Statistics Report," March 9, 2010, 2, 4–5.

46. Ibid., 4.

47. Center for Disease Control, "Health Disparities Affecting Minorities," www.cdc.gov/minorityhealth/brochures/AIAN.pdf.

48. Upton Sinclair, *The Jungle* (New York: The New American Library Inc., 1906), 198.

49. Associated Press, "Bangladesh Factory Collapse Blamed on Swampy Ground and Heavy Machinery," *Guardian*, May 23, 2013, www.theguardian.com/world/2013/may/23/bangladesh-factory-collapse-rana-plaza.

50. BBC News, "Rana Plaza Collapse: Primark Extends Payments to Victims," October 24, 2013, www.bbc.co.uk/news/business-24646942.

51. Benjamin Powell, "In Defense of Sweat Shops," Library of Economics and Liberty, June 2, 2008, www.econlib.org/library/Columns/y2008/Powellsweatshops.html.

52. Benjamin Powell, "Sweatshops in Bangladesh Improve the Lives of Their Workers, and Boost Growth." *Forbes*, May 2, 2013, www.forbes.com/sites/realspin/2013/05/02/sweatshops-in-bangladesh-improve-the-lives-of-their-workers-and-boost-growth/.

53. Tom Orlik, "Rising Wages Pose Dilemma for China," *Wall Street Journal*, May 17, 2013, http://online.wsj.com/article/SB10001424127887324767004578488233119290670.html.

54. Hunter Baker, "Reflections on Social Justice, Government, and Society," *Journal of Markets and Morality* 15, no. 1 (Spring 2012): 143–59, at 148.

55. Ibid., 148–49.

56. James C. Collins and Jerry I. Porras, *Built to Last: Successful Habits of Visionary Companies* (New York: Harper Collins Publishers Inc., 2002).

57. Ibid., 48.

58. Ibid., 47.

59. Mackey and Sisodia, *Conscious Capitalism*, 12–13.

60. Jef Feeley and David Voreacos, "Merck to Plead Guilty, Pay $950 Million in U.S. Vioxx Probe," Bloomberg, November 23, 2011, www.bloomberg.com/news/2011-11-22/merck-agrees-to-pay-950-million-to-settle-u-s-government-s-vioxx-probe.html.

61. Mackey and Sisodia, *Conscious Capitalism*, 50.

62. Matthew Herper, "Merck Could Return to Greatness if CEO Can Leave His Own Past Behind," *Forbes,* April 17, 2013, www.forbes.com/sites/matthewherper/2013/04/17/merck-could-return-to-greatness-if-ceo-can-leave-his-own-past-behind/.

63. Gallup, "Confidence in Institutions, 2013."

64. The informal economy is economic activity outside government supervision and management. Economist Hernando de Soto writes about the informal economy in his seminal work, *The Other Path* (New York: Basic Books, 2002).

65. Brooks, *Social Entrepreneurship*.

66. Noga Leviner, Leslie R. Crutchfield, and Diana Wells, "Understanding the Impact of Social Entrepreneurs,"Ashoka, 2007, www.ashoka.org/sites/ashoka/files/UnderstandingtheImpact ChapterPDF.pdf.

67. Alan Clark, "Why Big Business Should Support Small Business," Business Day Live, November 27, 2013, www.bdlive.co.za/opinion/bdalpha/2013/11/27/why-big-business-should-support-small-business.

68. Alex Forrester et al., "Praxis: Accelerating the Next Generation of Christian Social Innovators," The Gathering 2013, audio, September 30, 2013, www.thegathering.com/conference/audio-podcasts/2013-conference-audio-podcasts/.

69. Ibid.

70. Rising Tide Capital, "The Need We Fill," www
.risingtidecapital.org/index.php/about-us-16/our-approach/
the-need-we-fill.

71. Rising Tide Capital, *2012 Annual Report* (Jersey City, NJ:
2012), 3, www.microtracker.org/userFiles/520be8c02b6003113
7000000/Rising%20Tide%20capital%202012%20Annual
%20Report_web.pdf.

72. Ibid.

73. Rising Tide Capital, "Outcomes," www.risingtidecapital
.org/index.php/about-us-16/our-approach/objectives-
and-outcomes.

74. Forrester et al., "Praxis: Accelerating the Next Generation
of Christian Social Innovators."

75. Jacqueline Novogratz, "Making a Case for Patient Capital,"
Bloomberg Businessweek, October 20, 2011, www.businessweek.com/
magazine/making-a-case-for-patient-capital-10202011.html.

76. Microcredit Summit Campaign, "About the Campaign,"
www.microcreditsummit.org/about-the-campaign.html.

77. Gary Woller and Robert Parsons, "Assessing the Community Economic Impact of Microfinance Institutions," www.
microfinancegateway.org/gm/document-1.9.28984/49.pdf.

78. Amy Karzin, "Andhra Pradesh to Curb India Microfinance," *Financial Times,* October 14, 2010.

79. Karen Macours, Patrick Premand, and Renos Vakis,
"Transfers, Diversification and Household Risk Strategies:
Experimental Evidence with Lessons from Climate Change
Adaptation" (working paper no. 8940, Centre for Economic

Policy Research, London, April 2012), 9, http://dev3.cepr.org/meets/wkcn/7/789/papers/Macours_DP8940.pdf.

80. Macours, Premand, and Vakis, "Transfers, Diversification and Household Risk Strategies," 4.

81. United Human Rights Council, "Genocide in Rwanda," www.unitedhumanrights.org/genocide/genocide_in_rwanda.htm.

82. Arthur Brooks, "Earned Success," The Road to Freedom, http://arthurbrooks.aei.org/learn/earned-success-2/.

83. Arthur Brooks, *Who Really Cares* (New York: Basic Books, 2007), www.amazon.com/Who-Really-Cares-Compassionate-Conservatism/dp/0465008232.

84. Brooks, "A Formula for Happiness."

85. Acton Foundation for Entrepreneurial Excellence, "Three Magic Seeds," 2009, www.actonguides.org/pdf/3-Magic-Seeds.pdf.

86. Judith Warner, "High-Status Stress," *Time*, March 12, 2012, http://content.time.com/time/magazine/article/0,9171,2108019,00.html.

87. We recognize the question regarding the authorship of Ecclesiastes and whether it was written by Solomon or someone writing as if he were Solomon.

88. Elizabeth Dunn and Michael Norton, "How Money Actually Buys Happiness," *Harvard Business Review* Blog Network, June 28, 2013, http://blogs.hbr.org/2013/06/how-money-actually-buys-happiness/. They have also coauthored the book *Happy Money: The Science of Smarter Spending* (New York: Simon and Schuster, 2013).

89. Brooks, *Who Really Cares,* 150.

90. Ibid., 143.

91. Anthony M. Grant and Alison Leigh, *Eight Steps to Happiness: The Science of Getting Happy and How It Can Work for You* (Victoria, Australia: Victory Books, 2010), 70.

92. Lalin Anik et al., "Feeling Good about Giving: The Benefits (and Costs) of Self-Interested Charitable Behavior" (working paper, Harvard Business School, Boston, MA, 2009), 10.

93. Peter had the opportunity to attend and hear Shah speak.

94. Chris Heath, "The Unbearable Bradness of Being," *Rolling Stone*, October 28, 1999, 72.

95. Brooks, "A Formula for Happiness."

96. "Hope Springs a Trap: An Absence of Optimism Plays a Large Role in Keeping People Trapped in Poverty," *Economist*, May 12, 2012, www.economist.com/node/21554506.

97. Chandy and Gertz, "With Little Notice, Globalization Reduced Poverty."

98. "Towards the End of Poverty."

99. Mackey and Sisodia, *Conscious Capitalism*, 263.

ACKNOWLEDGMENTS

We're incredibly grateful for the team of people who have journeyed with us while we completed this project. Without this team, it would have been a different book.

We would like to thank Josh Good, Tyler Castle, and Meredith Schultz for your belief in this project and your clear guidance along the way.

We would like to thank our families: Alli and Laurel, your insights and conversations have changed the way we think about calling and vocation. Thank you for encouraging us to pursue the work we love. We clearly married up. I (Chris) would like to thank my grandfather, Abe Horst, and father, Bill Horst. From a young age, I learned by their model how to serve communities well in and through business.

Anna Haggard, you serve with joyful enthusiasm. Thank you for your editing, researching and writing, which dramatically impacted this book.

Andrew Wolgemuth, you are skilled at what you do, and you have been a faithful friend, guide, and advocate as our agent. Finally, we appreciate your always insightful advice on how to improve our work.

Christy Sadler, Claude Aubert, and the editorial and design team at the American Enterprise Institute, you are talented and insightful, and we're thankful for your graciousness and guidance throughout the writing and layout process.

We would like to thank Adrian Groff and Elyse Bealer, who were willing to personally share their stories with us.

To the reviewers who sharpened our arguments, we are grateful: David Bronkema, Amy Sherman, and Bob Lupton.

Special thanks to Steph Walker, Conrad Bess, Sean Williams, and Ryan Piesco, who wrestled with our text to provide insights and to improve our work.

To our Lord and Savior, your grace changes everything. *Soli Deo Gloria.*

ABOUT THE AUTHORS

Chris Horst is the vice president of development at HOPE International, where he works and writes at the intersection of entrepreneurship, work, and the Gospel. He is published regularly in *Christianity Today* and is coauthor of *Mission Drift*. He serves on the boards of the Denver Institute for Faith & Work and the Colorado Microfinance Alliance. Horst graduated from Taylor University with a business degree and has an MBA from Bakke Graduate University. He lives in Denver, Colorado, with his wife, Alli, and son, Desmond. Horst blogs at www.smorgasblurb.com.

Peter Greer is president and CEO of HOPE International, a global nonprofit focused on addressing both physical and spiritual poverty through microfinance. He has a master's degree in public policy from Harvard's Kennedy School. Prior to his education at Harvard, Greer served as managing director for Urwego Community Banking in Kigali, Rwanda, for three years. He also served as a technical adviser for the Self-Help Development Foundation (CARE Zimbabwe) in Bulawayo, Zimbabwe, and worked as a microfinance advisor in Phnom Penh, Cambodia. Greer speaks and writes on the topic of faith and international development and is the coauthor of *The Poor Will Be Glad*, *The Spiritual*

Danger of Doing Good, and *Mission Drift*. He and his wife, Laurel, have three children and live in Lancaster, Pennsylvania.

The American Enterprise Institute

Founded in 1943, AEI is a nonpartisan, nonprofit research and educational organization based in Washington, DC. The Institute sponsors research, conducts seminars and conferences, and publishes books and periodicals.

AEI's research is carried out under three major programs: Economic Policy Studies, Foreign and Defense Policy Studies, and Social and Political Studies. The resident scholars and fellows listed in these pages are part of a network that also includes adjunct scholars at leading universities throughout the United States and in several foreign countries.

The views expressed in AEI publications are those of the authors and do not necessarily reflect the views of the staff, advisory panels, officers, or trustees.

CHECK OUT THE OTHER TITLES IN THIS SERIES